"This is a joyous book. Even addressing unquenchable longing and the shadows of death and failure, the lyric engines of these poems propel us with vital combustions. Operatic, in that suffering and sadness are sung with the same gusto and octave-expanse as triumph and discovery, this work is proof of the presence of a large, funny and indefatigable spirit."

—Dean Young, author of *Shock by Shock*;
*Elegy on Toy Piano*, finalist for the Pulitzer Prize;
and numerous award-winning books

"Di Prisco mixes the immiscible: an authentic lyric voice and a sense of the self (and world) as dispersed and constructed. His poems are funny, smart, and moving; they quiz the options they exercise but are never coy."

—Guy Rotella, author of *Castings*

# SIGHT LINES FROM THE CHEAP SEATS

# SIGHT LINES FROM THE CHEAP SEATS

*Poems*

## JOSEPH DI PRISCO

THIS IS A GENUINE VIREO BOOK

A Vireo Book | Rare Bird Books
453 South Spring Street, Suite 302
Los Angeles, CA 90013
rarebirdbooks.com

Set in Minion
Printed in the United States

10 9 8 7 6 5 4 3 2 1

Publisher's Cataloging-in-Publication data
Names: Di Prisco, Joseph, 1950-, author.
Title: Sight lines from the cheap seats : poems / Joseph Di Prisco.
Description: First Trade Paperback Original Edition | A Vireo Book | New York, NY; Los Angeles, CA: Rare Bird Books, 2017.
Identifiers: ISBN 9781945572524
Subjects: LCSH Poetry, American. | BISAC POETRY / American / General
Classification: LCC PS3554.I67 S54 2017 | DDC 811.54—dc23

*To Aidan, Damon, & Kenna*

# ALSO BY JOSEPH DI PRISCO

### Poetry
*Wit's End*
*Poems In Which*

### Memoir
*Subway to California*
*The Pope of Brooklyn*

### Novels
*Confessions of Brother Eli*
*Sun City*
*All for Now*
*The Alzhammer*

### Nonfiction
*Field Guide to the American Teenager* (with Michael Riera)
*Right from Wrong* (with Michael Riera)

# TABLE OF CONTENTS

# PART ONE

# MY LAST RÉSUMÉ

When I was a troubadour
When I was an astronaut
When I was a pirate
You should have seen my closet
You would have loved my shoes.
Kindly consider my application
Even though your position is filled.
This is my stash of snow globes
This is my favorite whip
This is a picture of me with a macaw
This is a song I almost could sing.
When I was a freight train
When I was a satellite
When I was a campfire
You should have seen the starburst
You should have tasted my tomato.
I feel sorry for you I'm unqualified
This is my finest tube of toothpaste
This is when I rode like the raj on a yak
This is the gasoline this is the match.
When I was Hegel's dialectic
When I was something Rothko forgot
When I was moonlight paving the street
You should have seen the roiling shore
You should have heard the swarm of bees.

# MORE ELEMENTS OF STYLE

*I forgive everyone and ask forgiveness of everyone. OK? Don't*
*gossip too much.*

*Perdono tutti e a tutti chiedono perdono. Va bene? Non fate*
*troppi pettegolezzi.*

—Cesare Pavese's suicide note, 26 August 1950

"Hopefully" is an adverb meaning "full of hope."
You may write "You hopefully received the thousand red roses"
If you're dating the New Year's Day Parade in Pasadena.
Omit needless words except for *susurration* and *gash*
*Gold-vermilion.* Hold nothing back. Spend every cent.
Next morning, look hard at what you have left behind.
You'll be surprised—if you're like me, and you're not—
At the missed opportunities and water marks on the page.
Avoid inert gasses and verbs. Having is over-rated,
And being only goes so far, not that I need tell you.
There's no such thing as re-writing, you know,
Only writing. That's about as helpless as I can be.
Don't be discouraged when the piano tuner stops to eat
His hero sandwich over the keys. It's all part of the process,
A messy fugue. You are in this way one with
Everyone who ever penned a word. Sometimes,
Words like loved ones fail you, it's not their fault.
Sometimes you fail them, and it is.

Before long you may hear the piano chords played
In a far-off room, and you may feel a sadness
That lights within, a candle inside a carved pumpkin
All Hallow's Eve. This is normal. You're not, and no one is.
Sometimes the best writers break all the rules,
They make comma splices sing, they don't know they are
The best writers, and they just can't wait around to find out.
May I commend you on your use of concrete language
And your personal voice, petals on a wet black bough.
Read your work out loud, to others, or to yourself,
For you must listen to the music, the echo, the ping
Of conviction like a sonar signal under the sea.
Some nights are a sea and we are all submerged.
The moon makes tides, the man you are walks
A new shore and leaves footprints that are never erased.
Do not overstate, do not explain, be emphatic at the close.
This world is not for everyone, that much is unclear.
The other world calls out, saying come home,
You will be welcomed, there's nothing more
Hopefully left to be said, gash gold-vermilion.
Make sure your reader knows who is speaking to whom.

# THE RINGLING BROS BARNUM AND MY FAMILY
# CIRCUS

Bengal tigers don't naturally leap through rings of fire,
They must be trained, they must be abused,
Unlike my brother, who held the hoop and leaped
At the same time as if he had been born to do that
And he was. I myself am the Bearded Lady
Because there were no volunteers,
Which was all right, given the epaulets
That graced my dress blues. Animal rights activists
Make a good point. Don't tase Dumbo,
You slimy circus bastards, or my brother,
Who would not shoot you with a real gun.
My mom walked the tightrope with balance beam,
How else to reach the other side?
My dad was impatient below, arms folded, in case.
People fear the clown, but clowns are terrified of them.
Their cars run in circles, on pharmaceutical fumes.
Saturday my family circus showed for the funeral,
A regular stop on the tour. Smell of popcorn
Filled the air, like Iowa, cotton candy bloomed
In everyone's tiny hands like cherry blossoms,
A tornado touched down, the big top exhaled.

Rome: such a great city for walking unless
You are hit by a car, as I was tonight, though it was only
A tiny car. The cretino driver had my language progress
In mind as I practiced my idioms and gestures,
Like what they call "holding the umbrella"
(don't ask, think about it). The driver's eyes
Told me I had a long way to go if I wished to
Score a point about livestock and his love life.
Still, a sorrowful ghostly city like Rome is good
For dying if it came to that, so many spaces
For monuments, someday maybe one of Me in Language
School, in full command of the imperfect subjunctive,
Which is called the Congiuntivo Imperfetto,
Which sounds like a coffee or pasta but is not.
Later this night a girl in a piazza swathed in moonlight,
Unlit cigarette in her fingertips, asks in her English,
"Have you a fire for me?" Sometimes even Italian fails.
You won't believe how much you use the Congiuntivo
Imperfetto during foreplay, painting a ceiling, or when hit
By a car. Night times I spent in the Piazza dell'
Orologio—*orologio* means clock—sweepingly
Subjunctive and imperfect, and studied the big clock
On the tower, the one with missing hands,
And appreciated anew Italians' conceptions of love
And death and why they were always late.
I am the oldest student in the class by a factor of two.

Also the only male, by a factor of no idea. The Russians
Have atrocious accents but their grammar and miniskirts
Are exceptional, especially with the subjunctive mood.
The goal is to think in Italian, to speak without
Thinking, so I am halfway home. Maybe it was my toga
That turned the teacher against me. I ask her to go
With me to the Coliseum, where everyone soon dies,
As I will, which is why I first came to Rome.
The most beautiful girl in school is from Algiers.
Her black eyes demand I re-examine my whole life.
Oh, the things I could tell you about language school
Would fill a book, a little grammar exercise book
Specializing in the imperfect subjunctive, required
Every minute in Rome especially while sitting next
To a gorgeous sweet Algerian girl named Sisi,
Which in Italian sounds like *si, si*, yes, yes.
That's why, if I have to live, Rome is not so bad,
It's such a sad city, with the best art over my head,
Cars so small that afterward I run back to language school.

Your first dog is ever your one dog
And no story has a happy ending anymore.
We have all wasted lives, sometimes we waste
Our own. Some nights are long ones, some
Never end at all. I don't know how we can
*fall* in love, which implies landing,
Whereas love promises everything but.
That's why I like to listen to birds call
At dusk to each other from the acacias
But then I recall it's still daylight and I
Hear them in the absence of the trees.
When I am traveling by train over mountains
All I think of is the sea. My father was
Never quite so alive until he died and now
He's immortal. Somebody must do the calculus,
Somebody must work out the logic of the logic
Of this spectacle because spectacle's the last
Word anyone would use for dreams that don't cease,
For the sound of weeping coming from the next room,
Only there's no next room and we're the only ones
There, though just for a moment and a lifetime more.
Listen, I will tell you a secret, the secret you told
Me once on the train into the mountains
On the journey to the shore, a time long ago when
We spoke and never met. *That* secret, which is ours.

Some nights are so long the old dog comes home
To us who remain there waiting and waiting
Even if we've never been here before, where we are.

## SLEEP IS/IS NOT A LOST CAUSE

I needed new sightlines from the cheap seats.
Travel had to be sweeter than the night
Glued to the lampshade inside my head,
Since the knockout in the first round.

Soon I'm jetting to Rome, fondling strangers
Securely bereft of their expensive clothes.
I'm ordering the tripe, the oxtail, the brains,
Washing it down with caldrons of grappa.

That's why I count on being seriously sick.
The world is a strange place, that's for sure.
I can't subscribe to the existence of space
Aliens, though, I've been hurt before.

Tough to read *The Divine Comedy* on a Vespa
Or write it. If Dante drove a Vespa the history
Of the world literature would be revised.
Can't help I'm singing some aria, drunk.

Let's suffer blackouts together, boygirls and gargoyles.
Now the stars swirl in the whirlpool of
The looking glass. Cannot wait for day to break
Inside my diving bell, cuttlefish cling to the spire.

# LADY, WITH HIPPOPOTAMUS

Seems one night slipped the hippopotamus
Into her home and next day was Christmas, too.
In other news they exhumed Neruda while
A quartet played stately music on the sands of
Isla Negra. Officials wanted to determine for sure
If he'd been poisoned, but tests came in no.
Belief is a Chinese firecracker popcorning in
Your grasp. About that woman: she was smart
And she blew on pinwheels at every chance
And put her shoes in the oven to sleep
And showered twice a week in her pink PJs
If we didn't catch her first and she moved fast.
She had early onset dementia and apparently now
That hippo. We loved her and she loved Christmas
So I told her I wanted a pony this year.
She said she'd see what she could do, but first
There was a jittery hippo in the living room, which
Would get in Santa's way on this mid-summer night.
Let's review. People wire cash to a Nigerian prince
Exiled in London with email so as to claim
A fortune in misplaced diamonds and some fall
In love with serial killers on death row so don't
Give me grief about her one measly hippopotamus
Or Neruda's resurrection or Three Wise Men at the manger.
That was the night she called the police about the hippo.
After silence long as Saturday lines at the DMV

They dispatched a squad car and two cops.
Long-term memory being the marbly vault it is,
Once upon a time she'd been a professor, so she got
A broom and prodded the hippo into the corner,
The way she dealt with department rivals before.
In a zoo a hippo looks lazy and slow, jolly and
Oafish as a cartoon. Not so in the jungle.
That huge herbivorous mammal runs faster than you
And will bite off your head and shoulders if you come
Between it and a calf, and river bottoms are strewn
With the wreckage of boats that dared interrupt
A morning swim. Nobody at the academy had
Trained the cops to confront a lady like that's
Hippopotamus, and there it was in plain sight—
Only they had another name for her hippopotamus.
They called it a *possum*, which was close enough.
So they moved around chairs and boxes and made
An escape route out the front door. It took a while
But then they shivered as the possum snarled
And hissed, pink tail twitching, when it scurried
Out into the clear Christmas Eve night air.
That done, she asked the nice officers to help
Her find and decorate a tree. There were
Presents to roast and cookies to paint
And carols to string up and lights to sing
And oh yes, a pony to buy at the pony store.
But the cops were sorry, an elephant was loose nearby
And that was OK, she had the rest of her life
To get right what was always now a little bit wrong.
Merry Christmas to all, leaving her they cried out,
And to all in a brain blizzard good night, good night.

## EULOGIST ON CALL

Some kind of world it was it was.
So here is that fallen leaf lake you dream
All next day you dreamt, the dream
That shakes you out like liar's dice.
Yes, we're all unhinged, but some of us
Are doors. We gather by that lake
Where skittish palominos drink, where
Raptor shadows on the hillside fly.
Ripples running on the surface:
Unread pages deckle-edged.
There is nothing left to explain.
The piano drifts on lily pads. Who put
The harvest in the barn is immaterial
As am I. Long are the orchards,
Hollow is the house with echoing steps.
Here it is always autumn and the coats
Are perfect and you're ravenous not for food.
It's true a terrible mistake's been made
But it's not the one you thought. Nobody born
Ever had a Plan B, this was not your fault.
I see your face sketched upon the lake,
And water has become your last name.

Snapping on latex gloves clears the mind,
And lives of mystics are overrated, though not by me.
You need to define problem, need to define porn.
The world is Christmas-treed with pixels
And pop-ups, let's have a look. Desire is visual,
Maybe a new pill will again make me blind.
That time in Pompeii I got lost in the brothel
Where the saved frescoes depict menus for
The doomed, don't I know it, before the great
Eruption, when people swam in lava, choked down
Clouds of dust. Western Civilization, I rest
My case. Is that your handy Catullus or are you
Begging for it? I did not fail Philosophy One
Oh One for nothing, I failed it for everything.
Everybody's talking about zombies once more,
The nutritional benefits of flax seed and kale,
The balance achieved through Tai Chi.
I'm not here to argue about the body, I'm not
Here at all, I'm there, in the clearing, a risky place
That's not a place and the body is a beautiful thing,
Not that it's a thing. I'll tell you what happens to
Time, but not now, now I'm pulling out knives
From my eyes, now I'm tracking down my breath
From the snow summit. Before I was disembodied
The klieg lights unforgave me, afterward
I poked my head up through the recollected rubble.

The body is a factory, an internal combustion engine,
An electrical network and a jeweled temple, a planet
And a satellite with alternate day parking.
Monks and their out-of-body experience—nice work
If you can get it. Shakespeare the Bard thought love
Located in the liver, OK history's cruel, he also called
Ejaculated semen *spirit* so he's being unhelpful
For a change. Mind and body may possibly exist
Along a continuum, Philosophy Menage a Two-ah.
The Amazon River's kind of a continuum
With predatory fish and neonized birds and hostile
Indigenous tribes that thwack your kayak from
The banks, so hold that thought. Along about
Now I can almost hear somebody posit the soul:
This party must be coming fast to a close.
Some bodies are luminous, some gauzy numinous.
If you want to talk dirty, I will completely understand.

Garbage strike in Napoli, bella bella Napoli.
Castel Nuovo, drone of flies, orange-egg-yolk-sun,
Life is perfetta, quasi. Someone's broken into song,
Chances are it's me, threatened be the throng.
Strangers exchange reckless wedding vows,
Small arms fire, black market currency, cheese,
They can't shout down my "Nessun Dorma," it's Napoli.
See, the reason there are garbage strikes is that
Kingpin mobsters have lost their way. Skins
Of bananas and wine bottle shards make them want
To kill each other some more—you know, *mobsters*?
Meanwhile, fortune tellers in turbans set up shop.
He will get the corner office, she will find
The lost cat safe under her bed. They predict success
For me, just not in this lifetime or in Napoli.
I will, despite myself, endure for one moment
Impossible joy. I decree: Garbage strike, over.
Gangsters, seize brush and canvas, your black beret.
Fisherman, drag in the haul of your crustaceous life.
Where'd this red Vespa come from? Like I care.
A shimmering fish with a death wish turns into my soul mate,
Wraps her evolutionarily mixed-up mitts around my eyes,
We zoom through trash into the soup that's the sea.

## THERE COMES A TIME THERE COMES A TIME
*OR:*
## GO FORTH

Never order eel in a bistro with your girlfriend
In a land once called France thirty-five years
Ago when afterward you make a solemn vow—
Acid, never again. For certain that's the night
Van Gogh MRI'd the sky, thirty-five
Years, a minute, ago. I'd lost touch with her
And the continent since then. You know,
My investment banking career, Constance
And my four rug rats and pugs, keeping up
With the Fractals, the movie moguls next door.
College is a time to take risks, to work hard,
To eat an eel in France with your girlfriend,
Who's fucking half the Sorbonne,
While you scheme on the other half.
College was wonderful, I hear, and I have
One photograph of her for proof.
Never did learn the college fight song
But I could fake it like some orgasms
I don't need to re-visualize. About
Her photo, she's still wearing the crimson
Scarf and would you believe her picture
Was still on my desk alongside the model
Train set when she left me a voice

Mail? Yes, time is a funny thing, but I still
Harbor a grudge against Daylight Savings,
Marching through the house to disarm
The bomb in each device. Why so many clocks?
And all set to the same redundant hour,
Which I chalk up to missed opportunity.
So tonight I know where she is (phone,
Voice mail), but not where I am anymore,
Which is oddly how I might prefer
My eel these days. She has not changed one
Iota. Me? Time works on me like water,
Leaving less and less and thankfully less
In its wake. When I listen to her voice
Mail, my ear opens up to let her slither
Phosphorescent inside, a nice look
On her. I think I will save her message
For the rest of my life, which I have already
Squandered, long after eel and starry night
And the whole hallucinogenic motif.
I'm glad we had the chance to share
This time together, kids, that's all there is,
No really, that's all there really is. Nothing
Else on the court docket. Though true, I watched
That raptor soar a while against the setting sun,
A thus far uninhabitable earth-suck of a star
So thank you for inviting me to speak
At your commencement, it's been an honor.
Hook me up with grad parties, text me deets.
If you don't mind, all I've got is this Hazmat suit.

# DEFENSE OF POETRY?

*...the interlunations of life...*
—Shelley

Poets are also the unacknowledged contractors
Of the world. Lumber, electrical conduit, pipe,
Sheetrock, track light, double-pane glass.
We are a nation of flaws, here's to
Our foundry fathers. The Laughters of the American
Convolution. The canoes are not really dead,
They're resting. The lake laps against the side
Of the boathouse. Typical canoes. Tyler, too.
Down with slogans, once and for all.
When you find yourself in a poem walking at night
Don't automatically look to the guiltless seas.
This, we have done for centuries.
I have nothing against the ocean, though it seems
To have plenty against me. I refer to my
Astrological sign and the time the tide came up
When I played chess with the cormorants
Stuck out on a prómontóry which is accented on
The first and third syllables, which never feels right,
Does it? Which goes to the general point I'm not
Making. Give me the interlunations of life
Or give me death. One if by hand, two if on
Knees. The people have spoken, we have overheard.
What holds us apart is a thread of moon light.

Goodbye, locomotives and other motives, goodbye.
Moveable type, laptop computers, and quaggas,
Goodbye and goodbye. And goodbye, cantilevered
Bridge, goodbye, my tessellated childhood, bye bye.
Just pretend I know what I'm talking about.
Today, lurchings into reggae's lazy labyrinth,
Tomorrow, videophonic hookup with Tunisia,
Just like that we're surfing jeweled rosewater.
Been working on my theory. Her name is Lucille.
No, that's my guitar, goodbye. My new theory's name
Used to be the Human Genome. The Collected Forays
Of Shakespeare. I want to do with you, I want to do
With you what spring does weakening my knees.
I've consulted this big history of the cinema
And read myself into vacancies the historian left
Vacant, thanks, Historian. One day, Eminem will be
Gregorian chant. Once, there were those
Who believed in the existence of Jean-Paul Sartre.
We keep looking, goodbye, into the moue or the maw
Of the fashion model, assuming hunger would talk back.
No use bringing up when the elephants sang, goodbye.
The dinosaurs were killed by a colossal fiery metaphor,
so long. Online I read they found another dinosaur,
Hello? Today there are more dinosaurs than when I was
But a lad. Anyway, this dinosaur—pterosaur—had a little body
And big wings, making it a constant predator, watch out,

Much like those we dated in our subtracted youth,
So its extinction relates to the rudder that sprouted
Like a caliper from its head, as big as the rest of the bird.
Who can't sympathize? Goodbye, pterosaur, what's your hurry?
I forage in the ash forest seeking a flake
Of snow. I stumble across the anachronistic remote
And change the channels on the horizon.
From this porch of protein I marvel as to how
The streets are all swept clean in the dark.
I tag along with my trusty sidekick, Ciao, Bella.
The sidekicks have bid us all goodnight.

Robins eat fourteen feet of earthworms a day,
I've had a few run-on days like that myself.
Why not hook a fat comma on the recycling bins,
Staple semi-colons on telephone poles, air quotes
Around the flight pattern of a mourning dove?
The brace of clouds above cries out for the em dash.
Saint Crispin's Day, I cannot resist the urge
To assassinate the apostrophe. I fumble all night
In bed with a question mark, next morning stagger
On the circumflexed curb, my accent grave and legume.
I'll never again butt into a bar fight between two umlauts.
Please, what brackets you and me apart? Now it feels
Like @ sign six AM seems like parenthesis it's June.
Even the finches look exclamation point fatigued.
An avalanche of equal signs when rain falls a vector
On the just and just-so alike. Tuning fork surgically
Hyphenated in my blue-penciled head bullet point. I'm begged
To participate in a phone survey of my national mood.
Takes ten underscore minutes, says he slash she full stop.

# SYMPTOMATOLOGY

Now I'm a joke that works the first time and then
Never again. Can't help that I am ill.
I am sick. Under the weather. Off my feed.
Up to snuff, that's not me. I will never, long as I live,
Lick another handrail or rub my eyes with a chinchilla.
I am a microbial swamp, an airborne tumor,
Not OK, trending poorly. The ski-lift in my eyes
Is out of commission, a long line of miscreants
Waits with tickets to be punched. My hair? It's like that
To cover the surgical scars. Comparatively, scarecrows
Have upside. They said a pet would cheer me up
So I brought home a stray ventilator, now house-trained.
I swallowed a syringe. I devoured small arms fire.
I have a Richter scale attuned along my trigeminal corridor.
I submerged myself in a bath of after shave
And the tingling sensation reminded me how sick
I am. I need help. I am ill. I'm dabbling in black arts.
Witches, for a good time call. But you leeches, lay off.
Let me be unambiguous. I do not feel at the top of my game.
I am radioactive. I am prehensile, too, let that pass.
My condition is venereal, coronarial, vestigial,
And a little metaphysical, that's just how I am.
I am depressed and repressed, and my immuno-
Deficiency internal combustion engine is
Suppressed. I need to sleep. I need to hit the weights.
Scans reveal I might have experienced at some point

Fetal death. I am a felled tree and an Anglo-Saxon
Poem, I am sick. It was a lousy day when I learned
What goes into head cheese. Not that I need
Your sympathy, spare me. I'm living in a bubble,
Sorry I can't make the party, on account of my
Shingly leaves. It's caused by dirt I ate when I was
An irony-deprived child doing excavation in
The sand box, tra la. My eyes turn bluer by the hour.
There's the matter of an extra arm jutting off:
But it's nice to have back-up when I require
A flashlight to read directions to your house.
I've felt better. There's a spar in my chin, a spike in my toe,
An aquarium of Japanese fighting fish in my gut.
Hard to believe I once knew bliss. Once I pulled a sled
The length of the Iditarod, during the formative college years.
Yes, it's true. Once I even did dressage. This involves
A horse in a shocking way. Once I employed a valet.
He quit. Will you please help? You can't help.

# I WAS JUST LEAVING

Then again, I am always just leaving. It's the best part
Of showing up in the first place. The dog to be fed,
My kid to be picked up at the rink, a trip to pack for,
Anything to obtain clearance from traffic control.
These are not fabrications if somebody believes.
So long has passed since I was just leaving,
I almost forgot I ever arrived. So much ground
We have covered since. We wonder, what if we went
To one school and not another, turned down one street
Where the piano was lifted up the building side,
Missed the connection and the plane went down
In flames. Lives we might have lived, lovers
We might have betrayed or who betrayed us.
Sometimes I'm certain we missed the best times
Somebody might have had. And yet, and yet, who can
Forget the instant anesthesia kicks in—
*Ten, nine,* darkness—or remember it? And then
The black curtain is pulled back and we wake up with
A new knee, or a heart. That time I was just
Leaving was the time I did not, did not pass
By the casement window, descend the marble stairs,
Buttoned up my coat and walked out into the falling snow,
And reached up to pull down my hat against the cold
And realized I'd left my hat upstairs, where I still was.

# PART TWO

# BRIEF BIOGRAPHY OF AN IMAGINARY DAUGHTER

*Lonely as my desire is,*
*I have no daughter.*
*I will not die by fire, I*
*shall die by water.*
—James Wright

## #1 [COLLEGE]

We packed your satchel with sweatshirts,
Soccer equipment, and *The Elements of Style*,
Loaded up the Hum Vee, a sad drive to JFK
And the cross-country flight to starting college,
where fortunately due to Advanced Placement
Courses you've already been awarded your MFA
And published your first book.
As we pulled out of the driveway, I slammed
On the brakes, and not on account of Jubilation,
The neighbor's cat. "Stacey," I said, "we have jumped the gun."
"I didn't know we had a gun, Pops," you said.
"This is a figure of speech, a melonaphore.
But you can't go to college yet,
Stacey, you're barely by my count five years old."
"That's all right, Daddy-O, nice try.
But my name's not Stacey."

## #2 [PUPPY]

Love this puppy and your love will be repaid.
I can't stress how little this will teach you about life.
Which it will. Which is a lot.
Sometimes, when you're sad, I won't know what to say.
Desire will cut into the bone.
So much we need to cover before you're on your own.
This is a tea kettle, where goldfish won't feel at home.
When I was your age, before you were born,
A war was almost certainly about to break out.
The Russians turned out to be just like us,
Only worse drivers, which is a lot like us, too.
I had a pet once, too, you know. An accordion.
Very tough to train, stained with fluids as it was
About which nothing further need be said.
Your questions matter. No, they really do.
I have no clue as to the white carnations,
No reason to suppose the stars were not meant for you.

## #3 [FISH]

"Do fish sleep?" I am so glad you asked. Once
Upon a time fish did not even catnap.
Childhood has reached a certain point.

More specific than that, I cannot be,
Or less. When you drive to Chartres
You can see it coming at you far away.
Never pass up a cathedral if you can.
Drink lots of water with the strawberries.
Leap before you look too hard, which makes
Things swim in your head, like fish that never sleep.

## #4 [BIRDS...]

"Time's come to talk to you about the birds."
"And the bees?"
"What do you know about the bees?"
"Was just asking."
"A falcon is one bird you can't keep in a cage,
I can't explain why, though I might point
To history for many instructive precedents."
"You have trouble explaining, Dad."
"Anyway, what I like about birds is, they're much
Like dreams—they fly in through a window
Where you didn't know there was a window before."
"I get it. We open to the known and discover
Mysteries left in their place, like putting under the pillow
A tooth that fell out and you come up with the cash
When you need it in the morning, for school."
"Let's stay focussed, Amy." "Sure, Reginald."
"I mind it that you call me Reginald, who's he?"
"Someday, Dad, I may fall in love."

"Let's go back to the birds. I don't want to say
Love is for the ornithologists, though such thoughts occur.
Maybe the real topic is experience."
"I knew that." "When?" "You told me." "I never."
"Didn't have to." "That's how, you just know?"
"Life's a vale of tears, Pops, except when it's not."
"Hence, sweetheart, some birds thrive in cages."
"Name three." "I want you to try on some wings.
I want you to take flight. Like the day I gave birth..."
"What?" "The day I gave birth to you was the day of days."
"You feeling OK?" "The epidural worked like a charm,
I felt like I was swimming in air." "I think you're confused."
"I wouldn't be the first, but when they handed you to me
You nursed till you fell asleep." "You're talking about love."
"And some bees sting."

### #5 [BOND]

Once we had a bond, a sacred trust.
I carried you on my shoulders, we watched
The finches dart and feed, I read *The Odyssey*
To you, which OK was a stretch, but who cared
You did not exist? Certainly, not me.
But take the example of Homer.
Would you just give me a chance?
There's an old dog called Argus
Who waits for the hero to show before he dies.
I'm *getting* to the point. If we never had a dog

I would wait for you to arrive from a journey
Forced upon you by chance and fate.
You see, the whole thing's about waiting.
There you are off-stage readying yourself
For a grand entrance into a life none of us
Heretofore presumed. I myself ache
Barometrically in concert with the coming storms.
If you never are, I have something left over
Even if it's only me, watching you wade in, as if
You were a great swimmer and this world another shore.

## #6 [SORROW]

*Jamais de la douleur prendras-tu l'habitude.*
*You will never get used to sorrow.*
—Pierre Reverdy

Still, you can practice. Fire trails are good
As are Gothic cathedrals, mid-afternoon.
I say open a special bottle of wine.
I say asseverate by means of a Venetian mask.
When the circus comes to town, take to your bed.
If yours is not available, a friend's may have to do.
You will grow less unaccustomed to sorrow.
What is wrong with that contention? Use
The other side of the page to continue your essay.
The populace is divided, which is why we keep
The populace around. So often it is that we fall in love,

Why don't we just stop? I am thinking of a number
Between one and ten. Correct, the null set.
You can always meet someone at a cafe.
You can always memorize the periodic table.
How can anybody be drowning so far from the sea?
If you come by I'll bake you bread.
If you don't I will hover over the stew.
Vermicular is a word that sounds like what
It is (worms), whereas tumbrel and monger
Not so much. What was it you called to tell me?

#7 [CAREER]

OK, you want to be a poet, what can I do?
For starters, that's a rhetorical question.
Like when somebody takes the mic and asks,
Do I wake or sleep? Nobody's going to say,
Check aisle five, bulk goods.
Not existing already, you have a leg up.
Poets need emerald green hiking books,
A complicated country, Chile being a good example,
Red book shelves, a table cleared largely of
Snow, a badger, a very extensive wine cellar
And a great memory for clouds, streams, death,
Childhood, and dreams. Adopt a little lake,
Keep an eye out for the loons and their advanced
Academic degrees. If somebody comes up to you
After a reading and gives you a telephone number

You have taken a wrong turn. If on the other hand,
Somebody comes up to you, that's pretty good.
And excellent if somebody says, Goodbye, I love you,
I wish you had never been born, which is already
Fortunate as you know for you. And then somebody says,
I'll never write a poem like that if I live to a thousand,
But I'm glad you did, who knows when the plane
Departs, only you should be on board, listening to
The control tower as if these were undecoded secrets
Afloat in the jetstream between your ears. Careful!
Contents in the overhead bin may have shifted.
Finally, when the biographers touch down
And make crop circles, they'll be looking for signs
Of unhappy youth, negligent fathers, insensitive schools.
As if this is news and as if it matters. You're on your own
Here, as you always were and will be.
That's why you wear those emerald green hiking boots
And install the vista where you break the pledge
To settle down by a fire no one will ever douse.


#8 [GIFT]

I lost the pen you gave me,
The beautiful pen. For hours I overturned
Everything in the house. Nothing, nothing, and nothing
Some more. I called the stores where I shop.
They shared my grief. "I had a Mont Blanc
I lost once myself." This did not speak to my needs.

I looked one last place—your baby album.
There it was, the only thing inside: the pen.
It was almost worth losing it to feel so happy
To find it. Were I a Trappist monk who
Had renounced all earthly possessions
I would not have known such happiness.
It made me drive over to the Golden Gate Bridge
And almost fling myself into my sea.

#9 [RAIN]

What's in it for you?
On long nights, nothing but that question.
I do love the way the rain falls in June
When it's not supposed to rain.
We could wait in line for sushi or a symphony,
The tire repair, the prescription, or the bridge to re-open.
I want to go to the astronomy museum
And see the cranes nesting in Bolinas.
"A man like me" makes a lot of sense
Only when I do not, which is the case
During equinox, breakfast, and final exams,
Which have all been postponed. What's in it
For you? The sheen on a bird wing at dawn
When the dog is up already barking
Let me out! We stumble down the dark
Searching together for surprises left by the rain.

#10 [  ]

(Each emptiness yearns to be filled.)

#11 [CONCEPTION]

When you were conceived and I fell in love
The details need not detain us. Suffice it
To say, a lake may well have been involved.
And the unreliable car. So let me rule out during your
Formative high school years all lakes, all cars.
I'd like to take advantage of
Your never having been born
To remind you that you were
Never less than perfect even if
Imperfectly conceived. Child
Of my bitter old age, child of
My impecunious youth, child
Of refraction, child of prairie,
Wind, will you ever forgive me
For never having been? Will you
Sleep the half-life of swindled
Time and intentional accident?
Think of the rituals we can now
Re-invent. The death of one of us
Is still technically impossible.
Thursday will be our favorite day,
The early summer evening is prime.

I'm going to cook the food
You love, I'm going to read you
A long story for bed,
I'm going to keep my ear
Above your chest the whole night long.

## #12 [HOME]

When I came home you were not there.
At least you're consistent.
I ask the staircase, How was school?
You get the part in the play?
That's nice, I guess I reply to the stairs.
I'm going to paint the whole house
Tonight. Want to help your old dad?
I'll give you time to gather your thoughts,
Wherever you are tonight. Should have left
You dinner for before you met your friends.
Whenever I don't find you, it's not the same.
Maybe we could have watched some TV.
Only I see the set is gone, and in its place,
Is a blue cactus. Also gone, the couch, the chair,
The four walls, and the ceiling,
Which was something I never loved like you.

## #13 [PARADISE]

I'd like to take this opportunity to take
This opportunity to thank you for paradise.
The cars wave their semaphores,
The clouds are milked dry.
I am coming to the place
Where you and I part
For this is something I cannot yet do.
Your room is filled with carolers,
Your closet, with the menagerie.
I'm sending you a card
Postmarked paradise. So you'll know
How to find me, in the wake of the maple trees,
Stuck in the loom of the dark.

## #14 [MEMORY]

"My favorite memory: when you read me
Before bed. I was gifted recognizing the shape
Of letters, not so good, the meaning of words.
Fifty years later, the story remains the same.
I liked the one about the happy dragon,
Almost as much as the sorrowful duck."
"Once upon a time" makes me want you now.

But you're not here and it's not once upon
Anything. I'm working on the e-mail.
Working on the ladder. Working on the bee
That flew into my room. Once upon whenever
I missed you. Thought I saw you
Crossing the tracks near the house,
Carrying a backpack jammed with little dragons.
My own heart is a dragon foraging in a tiny field
Where the other kids break out the bats and gloves,
The cut grass where you lie, unable to wait.
I'm keeping those stories should you decide
To return. I'm learning the rest of my letters,
Stumbling on numbers greater than one.
Love is a fire a dragon brings on,
Love's at the tip of a falcon wing,
Tell me, just once, a story that's for you.

#15 [TIME]


I'd like to get on your calendar
So pencil in some face time for a few big talks
The books all say we have to have,
If you know what I possibly mean.
The sex talk. The college talk. The driving talk.
I'm sure you'll bring your own questions
To the table, even if we don't happen to own
A single flat surface, but let's not lose sight of
Losing sight of the real conversation.

Which is: I think blue is the best color for you.
I also don't think you're listening to enough music,
Or spending enough time alone in your room.
I wish you would not put all your stuff
Away when you're done or expend energy
Taking out the garbage. I've reassessed
Your dietary revolt: Maybe pizza and fries
Do constitute the perfect nutritional program.
Hope you give Chekov another chance,
He and I would do the same for you.
The report card came home from by the way
The school. I warned you about the trampoline
But I'm not going to go, I told you so.
I see you're excelling in Calculus,
Whatever that may be. And the study of ants
And the adjective Byzantine. A chip off
The old block, sweetheart, you surely are not.
Which is why I say blue, kingfisher blue.


#16 [SISTERS]


A credit card can be useful for restaurants.
No. No, that's what a fork is for.

Remember how I said I would always love
You unconditionally, that nobody would come
Between us? Not even if suddenly you had
A sister? She would be another person
Called a daughter I do not personally have.

Don't get like that, don't, please.
You're still my daughter in a manner of speaking,
One hundred percent. But you made me so happy
I could use with one or two more, and then I went,

One or two? Why not five or six, why not a thousand,
Why not a million more? In China and in India
They leave baby girls on mountain tops all the time.
You see where this is going better than I do,
Who have no clue. Which is what your new sister
Could be saying to you in the night when she shoves
Her way inside and cries, It's me.
And you go, I know, and when you touch her hand
The house turns into a minaret.

#17 [HISTORY]

Everybody's talking about empire.
Nobody's talking about my nasturtiums.
The candidates were beheaded in the square.
Shun all squares. It's impossible to avoid
Candidates. It is an illusion you were ever alive.
I was never alive, either. Well, there were
A few close calls. I recall the time I rose up
To address the throng and, what to my everlasting surprise
Should appear, hey, no throng. Just me in the place where
A throng is supposed to be. Which is a common
Occurrence as you yourself can testify.
There never is a throng when you need one.

And when you don't, of course, it's there,
As you take strike three, miss the shot,
Hit the wrong note, weep into the cold carrot
Soup. You would have loved my cold
Carrot soup. As a rule, rules are over-
Rated, but when it comes to soup, let her rip.
A soup takes patience. Takes time. You need
Soup to make soup, called stock, so
I'm glad you missed the war. That war
And all the others, too. When it was over
There was a new flag and a cortege,
Men stood on the platform and explained why
The platform would now be demolished.
See what I mean about squares?
I put the ocean outside your door.
Nice ocean, full of fish and water, of course,
Being an ocean. Sometimes, if you look hard,
A ship comes in, your name all over the bow.

### #18 [PLUMS]

Got your note when I woke at noon.
I'm doing more and more these days
Things I do not do. You said you ate the plums
In the ice-box that you believed I was
Probably saving for breakfast. "Forgive me,"
You wrote, "they were delicious, so sweet,
And so cold." Plums, I understand, but

Ice-box? Who taught you "ice-box"?
Forgot: I rescheduled your check-up
For Tuesday, after school. I don't like
That cough of yours, and let old Doc Williams
Look at the spider bite on your leg.
You could not have enjoyed the plums as much
As I savored your note, which I bet will
One day appear in the *Norton Anthology*
*Of Notes on Plums.* If I knew where to find you,
I'd plant leaky plum trees you could follow home.
Should have taken another look in that so-called
Ice-box. You'd have discovered the Mission Figs,
The Bing cherries, the Fuji apples, the pears,
The peaches, the canteloupe, and rambutans,
Which look like bristly strawberries
And taste like lychee nuts cross-dressed as almonds.
If you existed I would write you back and tell you
A mouth is a mystery that sometime must be kissed.
Someday you will love someone
So hard your stomach hurts, like there's a jacaranda
Blooming under your shirt. This is just to say.

# PART THREE

## NEIGHBORHOOD CLEAN-UP ODE: THE MUNICIPAL DIRECTIVES

*Do not place anything on top of dilapidated*
*Etruscan plinths.* The waste and detritus
Of the past twelve months: plunked on the curb.
I shove the word "detritus" into a banged-up banana box,
If you haven't used a shirt or idea for a year, toss it now.
I've dispatched the rumpled bed, my college French,
The oceanic color halfway between blue and green.
Ninety percent of the world's population lives one mile
From the shore. Throw this data point away right now.
So there's my expenditure for all to see on the street,
Like red-light window dressing on Amsterdam's quaint
Boulevards. It might be all right, Neighborhood Clean-up,
If I surrender busted books and TVs, and municipal gulls
Flocked and carried each shred of me off into the clouds.
For you have no notion what it was like to be hung over
A sitting duck in LAX and the X disembarks
Before your very bleating eyes, nor do I. But it's so,
And I fold that in bubble wrap, which qualifies as acceptable
Debris. If my door was dead I would hack it in half
Just as you require. Now's the chance to clean up my life.
Today I get rid of 2010, first part of '94, most of '91.
The time I engorged myself on the Nietzschean oeuvre.
The authentic shades of love, dried up house paint
In the can, an environmental hazard of the second degree.
Old instruments, begone—shepherd's crook, zither, stethoscope.

Things I don't need, things I let go, things someone please steal,
Only one thing's left won't let go of me: how loss is loss
Is loss is loss is loss is loss is loss.

Because later he has a tennis date.
He'd delight in a bowl of figs,
Your fatted calf, a bucket of balls.
These days, he likes a little company.
Take a shot if you can tell a joke.
The loneliness of a satrap is the hood
On his falcon, a goat on the side of a hill.
When he graduated first in his class
From Satrap School, was he a tent on fire!
Taxes to levy, rebellions to crush,
Aspiring maidens to bed.
They would feed him grapes, he'd shave
Their legs. He updated his threaded-gold
Caftans, he encrusted his shoes with gems.
Satrapping around took its toll in time.
His memoirs did not take off.
Nobody in Hollywood took his call.
Take the Satrap to Work Day was a bust.
Edicts were ignored, decrees, mocked.
He begged the dog to chase the ball.
The Saluki preferred the rabbit dream.
The Satrap will see you now,
Tomorrow he beheads himself in the square.

# WEDDING SEASON

The bride was Spring Break and the groom was called
Google.com. To the rotunda top rockets white doves,
Down go the Jell-O shots, Irish, and rum.
Desire wed Sincerity—who could see that coming?
And what a surprise, Cricket and Hummingbird.
Who would have counted on the hundred-strong
Harmonica marching band? Nucleotide and Glowworm.
Stock Option and Periodic Table. Precambrian Era
And Harley Davidson. Ship of Fools and In a Station
Of the Metro. Breast Stroke and Anterior Cruciate
Ligament. War of 1812 and Sonnet 129.
True, some pairings seemed inevitable.
Scar and Veil. Jealousy and Virgin. Tuna and Rye.
Spa Music and Deep Tissue Thai Massage.
Maine Lobster and Drawn Butter sent a save-the-date.
It was sad when Muse thwarted Poetry on the pyre.
Heartbreaking when Great White and Moonwalk
Flipped over the buffet and turned backs on in-laws.
But nothing rivals when Irony cheated on Post-
Modern as hip hop kicked in at the champagne bash.
Live long enough, and see? Sunday Brunch married
Gettysburg Address. I thought she appeared pale
And he'd prove nothing but a rant,
But look—I was wrong, I'll be going to the bris.
I've RSVP'd already to the wedding of
Middle East Conflict and Great Barrier Reef.

Something about weddings makes me want to plunge
Headlong into a tiered butter cream cake,
Entrust my car keys to the drunk valet.

# EMPEROR WITH NO CLOTHES

*If you care about yourself at all, come to your own aid while*
*there's still time.*
Marcus Aurelius 3.14

Citizen of Rome, you are the center of the universe.
Problem is, circumference is—take a guess—me.

"Some things are impatient to be born
While others are impatient to die." Don't say

I did not warn you. Next time they swear
Shit happens, pop them square in the nose.

This will not help anybody, but helping is
The farthest thing from my imperial mind.

If you keep your spirit blameless and pure
People will drape you with laurels but

No one will have sex with you in backseats
Or marble mausoleums or anywhere else,

A small price to pay for honor and respect
Though not for me, being an emperor with no clothes.

Just pretend today is the last day of your life
And act accordingly—not that such strictures

Apply to Yours Truly, sports fans.
The forces of evil march on the fortress

Of your self. I wish I could explain why.
But what if evil did not exist and what if

Your self was no fortress, see what I mean?
Stoics get a bad name. *Not in touch with feelings.*

*Too rigid. Know-it-all cocksure mothers.*
So the Stoics retain PR firms, don't tell a soul.

If you really knew what was good for you,
And you do, why do you care I'll flail you alive?

True, pissing off your emperor is a poor plan,
Even one like me mounted bare-assed on a steed.

Once upon a time, children… The story peters out.
Circus revels and gladiatorial raves—

Seen one, seem them all. Life is tiresome,
When will it end and will we ever notice?

I wish I knew. Really, I wish I cared.
My pal, Marcus Aurelius, natters day and night:

"Living is more like wrestling than dancing."
Guess he never saw me take Molly at the club.

And he says we always have the option of
Having no opinion. Right. Like he knows.

OK, then, where did I put my pants?

# TALK

Thank you for coming tonight. Like you
I tried to get out of it, but look,
Here we all are—well, those of you who
Aren't still killing time in the lobby
Hoping for a small earthquake,
Which, to be honest, I understand.
After I speak I will take your questions.
I bet they will be great questions,
I bet some of them will have already
Appeared in print, I bet you will
Dedicate your question to your spouse,
I bet I will disappoint one and all
But I promise afterward good wine.
You know how you're driving cross country
And you just mainlined a pot of bad
Coffee at the truck stop and you must get
To the coast in time for a father's funeral
That takes place in two days and gas is on F
And driver is on E? And the highway lines
Undulate like the *sin* function in trig class?
Well, my talk will be full of images like
That, you wait and see. I will read
Selected passages, please turn off your phones.
At the reception you may possibly conclude
If they invited me to speak there's hope
For you—or maybe just the opposite.

You are in luck because: no Power Point
In my bag of tricks. A, that's so Two
Point Oh. Second, I haven't a clue.
I will lighten the mood from time to time
With anecdotes and self-depreciating jokes
That amount to humble brag, which you'll
Sniff out, if you ever come in from the lobby.
There are still spots open at the front.
They asked me to talk about the new book.
If I could talk about it I would not have
Written it. We all know people who go on
And on about books they are writing and do not
Manage to write them. OK, that last point
Makes me sound like a jerk and my goal
Is you don't find that out first. Be on
The lookout for literary allusions and influences.
Later please tell me what they are, thanks.
But you'll probably ooh and ah about
The cowboy shirt and alligator boots—
Sorry, Ecosystem. Those of you in the lobby,
It's lovely up here behind the podium.
I have no idea how they will introduce me,
Someone, they'll say, who needs no introduction.
When I finish, books will be for sale, guess where?
In the crowded lobby. Unless the arsonists succeed.
One of you may find yourself I guess
Strangely smitten. Talks are where I met
All my exes, none of whom could attend
Tonight. Though I could, as you plainly see.
Now it's time to begin, then it will be time
For regrets. Next time, I promise to be better.

## OBSERVATIONS OF A FAILED THERAPIST

Hold on there, girlfriend, we don't talk like that
In here. Your loving mother had her reasons,
That's my analysis. So let's try again, shall we?
This time without the self-pleading, the injured
Merit, which is my patented personal go-to move.
Your world is full of contradictions? What was
Your first clue, Ms. Assistant Professor?
Oh, mortality, that is a bitch. Let's circle back
To something you mentioned, how you loathe me,
How I am a voyeur and a narcissist both.
I saw that coming, I didn't go to shrink school
For my health, you know. The technical term for your
Problem is transference, so it's predictable
For me to be loathed. And what *about* my scarf?
I have it on good authority it works with my complexion.
Perhaps seeing a female therapist *would* be indicated.
But I was thinking canine. I was thinking gnome.
It's all about you, isn't it, young lady,
And your precious crises, what about me?
A man has feelings, a man's going to die, too,
You know. A man can't always account for his
Whereabouts, his overriding despair and uselessness.
I see our time is up. Our time's been up ever
Since you first showed up in black boots and weeping.
No, please don't go. I'd like you to close
Your sea green eyes and free-associate a minute.

"Pathetic" is not an appropriate response. Has
Consideration been given to pharmaceuticals?
To even out my swings of mood.
I'm not ruling out brain surgery, I'm not
Discounting a career shift. Only thing in the way,
I'm just not sure you're ready to change.
Had this dream about you the other night.
We were in the choir loft and the water
Level was rising and rising and you spoke
To me in I think German, which normally
I don't understand and where were we going just now?

# HEAR YE, HEAR YE, LISTEN UP

During the great syncopation of King Mope Mope,
In the reign of the Cruciferous and Crustaceans,
The heyday of the Ho-ho and the year of the Pot Belly Pig,
There came to be either a census or consensus
When the moon waxed and waned above taffied templates
That had pillared us, pondered us, and pitied us,
In no particular disorder. A time of war it was
Like any old time at all. The people,
They gathered as people do in defiance of edicts
And of Dame Edith, who refused placation and oral
Surgery despite the delineated protocols.
When the sun fell into the sea, during the surge
Of the flippered and the flippage of the Megatots,
The tetrarch Manuel bullwhipped the oligarch
Oswald, who was used to such cowtowing by
The rashly incipient. Still, the word came down,
The marker was called, the field was plowed,
And thus it was that Philia's countenance shone
Upon the multitudes, who obviated it not.
Woe betimes, snipped the intubating respirators,
And a proclamation went out to all the outlier regions,
Ruled by the Regicides, potentates of possibility.
The voice of one lying in the wilderness:
Behold, the hour is come, the nigh is near.
Behold, all is forgotten but not forgiven,
The crooked is made straight, but straight

Has been tempered by a million fires stoked
In the belly of nought in the desert ops of cluelessness.
All would be made clear, all would become new,
Now that time had been dunked into a cold bath
And one may walk alone, shedding raiments
Like failed fashion hypotheses for the runways of Fall.
Take heed, for the lions, the vipers, the wolves
Are suppurating in the plazas of continuity.
That sense of expectation billowing within like the wind,
That is the conviction you have lived,
That despite all the evidence, you must go on
For a while longer, until the winnowing fork
Breaks on your tongue and the granary seeds
Scatter like so many beplunked notes.
Hear ye, listen up, this is the word from on high:
You must perforce gather your possessions
Along with loved ones and cross the closest river.
You don't have to be a loser in order to be found.
You don't need to be heard in order to cry for help.
You must be contemporaneous, though, to live.
Ascend the next mountain and suck in all the air.

# MY CONTRIBUTOR'S NOTES

*Awards*
Heterosexual Agenda Male Bias Runner-up.
Agronsky Wetlands Chapbook Champ.
Bicameral Grant for Sidereal Studies.
Honorable Mention Dissociated Poets Prize.

*Education*
Went ten rounds with a liposuctioned trombone,
Which is what I get for leading the marching band
Through Malibu. Memories of birth trauma and marriage
Turn crisper year by year, and I spun
A mean plate at my summer circus internship.
Somewhere I've got *magna cum nada* degrees
And crop circles, several leading Rockies,
The Houston Skyline and one half of Brooklyn.

*Publications*
My poetry has been tarred and minimally
Feathered, and I plagiarized the change jar
For beer after the off-campus reading last week.
Can't explain why teachers took a pass
On the résumé or why my long-delayed manuscript
Was barbecued to cinders in what investigators
Determined to be auspicious circumstances.
If only editors could read me. I will go on. They told me to.
Here's something almost considered by *Sports Illustrated*.

"My Love Life"
The NCAA tournament brackets have been at last
Announced. I'm looking for an underdog
To come through. A point guard

Who can set the tempo, who can make a mid-range
Jump shot, a coach who's good drawing up X's and O's,
Schooling the zone, and employing clichés.
All right, one time, she lost the handcuff keys.
Another time misplaced the egg beater,
Took a flyer on the French drain ooh la lah.
Basketball is a team game, it's about moving without
The ball, playing defense with her gorgeous feet,
About playing your game, staying within yourself
And sometimes within somebody else. Get an opening,
Go for the hoop. Take what the opposition gives you
And don't give it back. Some very good teams
Are always left out of the tournament, very hard
To say why. Basketball was invented in 1891
By James Naismith, a Canadian with two peach baskets
And thirteen rules. He wanted boys to have something
To do indoors during the long, long winter months.


*Current Project*
Inventing new sex games that do not require
Abject pleading. Otherwise, a spider took up
Residence in the corner. When the sun pours in
And the wind picks up, filaments glow like neon.
Please find attached said spider web.

# THINGS I NEVER SAID I SAID

I never said elephants sing when they mourn
Though I could have because it's true.
I never said scars would one day heal
Because how would somebody like me know?
I never really said I took your cumin,
Never said it looks like rain, wear a coat.
I never said I'd water your house plants
When you ran off to Mexico without me.
That I knew what you were going through,
Which is what *you* said to me, and maybe
It's the case I never said I'll never go to
The movies ever again or iron my white shirt
But I did say I stole your caraway seed,
Which you didn't even know you owned,
Which speaks volumes, yet another thing
I never said I said. You could write a book
On all the things I never said I said,
And I never said that, either.
I never said the gas tank was full
And the yoghurt was still good despite
The expiration date, never once said
I'd prefer cremation someday or possibly
Ever, that I was fixated upon death,
No, because that was you now in Mexico
Without your lonely house plants. Did not
Say I was falling in love with you,

Because I already had. That I'd bring home
Thai take-out, the pad Thai you love
Unlike me—you know what I mean—even when
I do not say what I never said I said. Never
Said I was a good dancer, either, never said
Sorry about that party, that I put my hand
On your friend's knee, except for one time.
And about losing your shoes at the wedding:
They were fantastic shoes and your feet
Looked so gorgeous enwrapped by those black
Straplets, but, being an idiot, missed my chance,
Which I never said I said, and you took them off,
A hot night in the Valley, and we all danced
Till I forgot I was dancing, more like breathing
Inside your lungs, which was the main thing
I never said I said because I couldn't believe that
Was the end of us, that night when your shoes
Disappeared. I never said I said I hated Mexico.
I never said I'm returning the cumin, but I did,
That I've watered your parched plants, so I'm
Saying them now, things I never said I said.

## THE BAR AT THE END OF SOME OTHER ROAD

Kind of place nobody's ever walked in for the soup.
You order the soup. Barkeep thinks he's famous and has
Bottle caps for eyelids and a girlfriend who cuts
His hair so when track lights flick, looks like
Broken glass rained on his head.

Place where it feels like a fight's always about to
Break out and you're in the middle.
Combustion, then silence oomphs like a blanket over a fire,
*Boom* from the back room like a flat tire, you doing eighty.
Kind of place lobster traps give up, hang a hundred miles
From the sea on the cork ceiling, fish nets limp on the walls.
If you stare too long at the baseball game on TV
You might go blind, a risk you'll have to take.

Where nobody talks to you and when they do
They stare straight ahead, like now with this girl,
Can't tell for sure if she's pretty or a girl, and she goes,
You new in town? Like she means it. Says
She's never seen you in here, which is
One true thing you both have in common.

Kind of place a girl like that gives you her name
And wind picks up and you see corn silos for days
And trucks, and dogs that would drag her out of
A burning car if they have to, which you can understand,

You might do the same, the least you could do. Now her name
Comes back: Elaine. Definitely rhymes with *Elaine*.

She asks who's winning. She means the game, but
You know better. The pearlescent white
Buttons on her cowboy shirt gleam like her perfect teeth,
The one thing perfect in this kind of place,
Where a bowl of soup is nothing you should count on.

# READ DIRECTIONS FIRST

Don't palpate ambivalent tangerines or breasts.
This just looks like an exit. Allow one minute to cool.
Three nasal applications under waterfall
Max daily. After opening, refrigerate.
Upon closing, oscillate. Refrain from
Checking tire pressure while operating vehicle,
Which may prove unsafe under certain
Conditions. Solving for X, don't forget Y.
Safety glasses advised. Nobody without hard hat
Allowed on work site. Shake well.
Pour carefully. Sing desperately. Wash before
Wearing in cold water with colors you like.
Elevate the legs, apply polar icecap melt.
Decant over candle, sauté till translucent.
Have a problem? Contact Customer Control.
When oxygen mask drops, there is not time
To answer the CEO's urgent sext message.
Put your tray in an upright locked position.
Levitate like this. Leave firearms at front desk.
Treat a corner of fabric first. Never
Connect ground wire during tsunami.
Restrict usage to daylight hours.
Wait while I check your account, this
May take a few seconds. In the meantime,
Hold on, could be your day. *That?* Nothing to fear,
Just somebody's lame idea for Halloween.

Forget your password? Check back Christmas.

Don't stick anything in my ear unless you mean it.

## NO ANIMALS WERE HARMED IN THE MAKING OF
## THIS POEM

Though llamas gobbled up the rhymes
And the camel spit on the box of ghazals.
Polar bear extras were fitted with cross-country skis
While seal pups splashed inside a wheezy villanelle.
And as for the great white sharks, I forced
Them to attend the dolphin relief benefit.
Horses mingled on the mesa with the surly unicorn
Without incident, and the black mambas
In economy were issued temporary library cards.
The chimpanzee unfortunately was pulled over,
Driving through a Yield sign and cited for
Transporting barbarically yawping macaws
Whose Tourette's Syndrome negatively impacted
The highway patrol officer. Meanwhile,
Lions balked about Pilates classes required
By the Code but the juggler did employ stunt
Doubles when working with the condor eggs.
Despite rush hour traffic the alligators crossed
The interstate and tickled the ear of the Jack Russell
Comatose on the veranda. I'm happy to report
Bunnies were cuddled by raccoons for a change.
When the Cooper's hawk shilling computer sales
Knocked on the cyberdoor with additional memory
Uploads, this came in handy, and when the tarantula
Pouted we needed stories to tell round the ol' campfire.

Now, I do need to concede humans were dinged up
In the making of this poem. A B-lister
On the lam smoked a baggie of speed-laced weed
And kissed the starlet till her lips glowed and glowed.

# THE OBSESSIVE-COMPULSIVE ATTENDS
## A COSTUME PARTY

With a turtle in my soup and a pill on my tongue,
With a beer in my scrubbed paw and a comet
In my urinary tract, with a cowboy hat on top
Of my conditioned head and a car that never starts up,
I left notes for the house sitter, just in case.

If the Pretty Jessica rose bush should bloom
While I'm gone, no need to panic and compose some ode.
PJ plays her little games, but keep an eye on that
Wily wisteria, which I just don't trust. If the rescue
Dogs whine, give them Critique of Pure Reason.

Let's say the jazz quartet mold in the cellar
Jams all night with sump pump and sheer walls.
Let's say the water pipes freeze and burst.
Let's say the street roils with a seven point one.
Let's say the Huns solicit for Vandal relief.

What if aliens near the barbeque pit descend?
Could be the night of the lunar eclipse,
Could be I'm registered to vote on nuclear waste,
Could be the fireplace glow won't die down,
Could be darkness falls like fruit from the trees.

Feel free to sit in any of the vanquished chairs,
To stock the cupboards with psycho-pharmaceuticals.
You can use the sheets, towels, and barbells,

But I wish you'd please keep out of my dreams.
I will be returning around the crack of dawn.

Don't smack the man in a cowboy shirt with
The cast-iron frying pan, try the tambourine.

## SOMEDAY I'LL GO BACK

Someday I'll go back someday
When no one's watching who cares,
Where the bike'll be chained outside
The ER someday. Somebody should
Go back, I still have the blue scrubs,
After I work up a good sweat
At the gym soon as the movie's over.
I'll go back someday first thing
After I re-hang the door,
Patch the holes in the walls.
That's when I'll go back,
When we got the dog at the pound
Before the asteroid shoved
The earth off its axis, blocked
The sun and dinosaurs blinked,
Before fish sauntered from the sea,
Back when docs smoked before
9/11 and the Gettysburg Address.
I'll go back someday, someday I hope
Someday, after rivers overflowed
And fires jumped the line I'll go back,
After the flyover and the drone drive by.
Someday I'll find the sparrow
That crashed into the window,
Lift it up and it will fly off, then
Someday I'll go back someday

When it's long after last call,
When if anybody has cause
Speak now or forever hold
Your peace, back to the time

When the stands were packed
And I threw the perfect pitch
In my mind and I'll go back.
I want to go back someday
Where babies come from someday
How penicillin was discovered
And the lost city of Atlantic
City, let me go back to where
I left my luggage and my keys
Which I never need now that
I need to go back the day someday
You asked, "Where'd you get the car?"
And I went, "From the shop", and you said.
"OK don't tell me," and I said, "Fine."
Let me go back when we drove
Till you glimpsed a lake below
And then you jumped out, undressed
At the water's edge and dove in
And it was dusk and you swam
Alone and I waited in the car
And I was the one submerged.
Someday I wish I could go back
To when trees riffled with your laugh
Looming over the lake, lucky lake,
And immersed you and also me
Someday I'll go back someday,
And find you onshore as if I'd

Never gone, then someday I'll go back
Someday back before this all began
When I'll go back someday, someday.
I'll go back someday, unlock
Your bike and ride away, away,
Someday, which is what I'll do
When someday I come back, someday.

A boy's first fifty years are quite precious.
I cannot stress enough how crucial Puccini
And the overhand curveball can be. That way
His knees won't buckle during *La Bohème*
When a curve ball starts out from behind his ear.
His first five decades of life can be pivotal.
Introduce him to the pleasures of the dunes,
The combustion engine, oh, and parabolas, too.
Give him names for birds and dreams of flight.
Show him death's card tricks so he won't be
Suckered though he will be which is why you do.
Teach him what money can't buy—both things.
Researchers confirm the theory, they ran tests.
They put the 40-year-olds in a canary cage,
The 30-year-olds on a South Seas atoll,
The 20-year-olds inside the computer's cloud,
The 10-year-olds in a kingdom by the sea.
Lab coats said dare to eat a peach. 'Tis not
Too late to seek a newer world and leafy greens,
To ruffle fringed epaulets in the marching band.
No need to join the men's reading group or build
A summer retreat, but I do think his hothouse
Orchids could stand a tweak and his dogs would like
To lie 'round a fire with him when he cracks the spine
Of a Jean Jacques Rousseau. Nothing finer than bow
And arrow on the fjords, a breakfast of shirred eggs

With a dollop of golden caviar. Timing, you roustabout,
Timing. Draw not to an inside straight. Sleep not
In a seal pup's skin.  Breathe not one word of golf.

# ANTHRO APOLOGY FIELD NOTES

*I hate traveling and explorers.*
—*Claude Lévi-Strauss,* Tristes Tropiques

We fail when we bring preconceptions as to the primitive
Mind, or assume ours isn't.
If I may continue.
Even so, for me, once is enough with a meal of bugs
In batter fried to a golden crisp. I prefer my bugs
Where they used to be in the jungle, sipping on my eyes,
Twisting parasitically in my ethnographer's guts.
Here they venerate vodka and Converse High Tops,
Tie garlands on crutches, put on crash helmets for bed.
Have stumbled on no arrowheads, bowl shards, or bones,
But note how dejected all their cars appear,
Like Russian kitchen appliances (sketches attached).
Their sex lives are rich with play and assault and battery,
And during early onset puberty, boys and girls could be heard
Once night fell in the forests, clicking their helmets.
I'd heard accounts of cannibalism but could not confirm
If they roasted or boiled or ran each other through a juicer,
Which is a controversial means of obtaining nutrients.
On every corner, chickens, pigs, goats, and ideas
Are being sacrificed to their gods, of which there are many,
None of whom have names that can be pronounced
Though all resemble armadillos with anteater tongues.

The females universally menstruate on the same night,
Which is when males run like Pamplona into the stadium,
Passions running high over the national sport,
Which, near as I can tell, is collective amnesia.
This extraordinary tribe cries out for more research
But it will not be completed by me, as here I've made
My new home. Once I heard the nuclear-collider-size
National tea kettle go off, signaling the incursion of
Enemy bands, who seized the movie houses first,
Then fell asleep during trailers, woke up and slinked
Back, popcorn in their beards, across the border. The whole
Country has one telephone, and when I picked up
It was always my ex, and her song was the same:
Wash off the face paint, unplug the nose and ear posts,
And return. Last night I heard the communal orchestra
Of metronomes, tuning forks, and freight trains
And caught myself yearning for somebody to show up quick
With the cracked ice and High Tops but not my ex.
The volcano is due to blow, I can feel it, my only refuge
The salty sea, my crash helmet, and my notes from the field.

## BEETHOVEN'S, FIFTH, SAN, FRANCISCO,

It was raining paisley umbrellas and we kept
Bumping into them on the swarmed sidewalks.
Most times I go to the symphony hall
Somebody just nods off and snores
Till he's poked in the ribs. Hope tonight
That promises not to be me. The 19th century
Is a very important century for music,
Factories, and novels that go on and on.
You think when Beethoven sat down at
The piano he was thinking 21st century?
I myself have been known to approach
An unsuspecting piano, the mood hits and night
Is coalescing around a few precious concepts
Too transparent to be delineated by such an
Unreliable aviator. Beethoven may have been
Insane, but then again that was so 19th century.
Dostoevski, etc. And let's not forget Nietzsche.
What always gets to me in the Fifth is
The sneaky melody line, the lilt in the air, a light beam,
How a field opens, like with too much moonlight
And pixillated pixels birthday-caking about
And moonlight is something of which
You can never have enough. When I
Was in school, it was considered bad form
To write a poem about a piece of music.
I still inscribe to this theory, though now I dispute

The word "about" in the phrase "about a piece
Of music," and now that I think about it,
Also "piece." "I find it pointless,"
Writes Igor Stravinsky, "and dangerous to over-
Refine techniques of discovery" in his book
*Poetics of Music*, which if you don't know
Stravinksy the way I don't know Stravinsky
You'd find hard to believe. Now the second
Movement of Beethoven's Fifth is really
Lush. I hate the word "lush" for reasons
Too belabored to be obvious. It's enough to
Make me leap to my feet and forget about
My colonoscopy, about which I pledge to add
Nothing further. Beethoven's almost too beautiful
To hear is what I'm trying to get around
Saying, but I'm still tracking down that part in
Stravinsky, and I'm giving up, hearing the oboes
And the strings call out, and I'm going with them,
And sure enough, somebody's snoring, but
At least it's not me with tight shoes kicked off.
In the 5th Symphony Beethoven gives us
A space to step back and wander alongside,
Figuring out what we are doing where we are,
And then, wham, back to melody and ta ta ta
TA!, electric wavelets on the brain's craggy shore,
I just can't get it, I don't know what to say

Except time speeds up not in a bad way like
Brennan's Bar, closing time, but in a we-got-next-
Game kind of way when we know we have the right
Mix of inside/outside. See what happens when the bird cage
Door flings open? That's the Fifth for you.

Deepak and I were flapping our gums about secrets
Of the universe. He's a guru, he thinks that gives him
A right. Actually it was more about the beer.
He was talking hops, he was talking water quality,
But the game was on TV so I'm not totally sure.
He was not the easiest roommate, as you'd expect.
Gurus don't wash their dishes or take out garbage,
They steal your shirts and girlfriends and later go,
"Was that your shirt or girlfriend? Sorry, man."
He's probably levitating somewhere by a hot spring
Now and I don't miss my shirts or girlfriends
As much as I miss him. Deepak taught me a lot.
Like, peeling a hard-boiled egg requires
Spiritual discipline, hand-eye coordination,
And having a hard-boiled egg. Time was,
My universe was devoid of eggs and purpose.
I don't like going to New Year's Eve parties
Anymore, especially those I'm not invited to.
The fancy parties feature bubbly and caviar,
Which is sturgeon eggs, served with chopped
Onion and still more eggs, so no thanks,
I've had my fill. Think I'll watch the ball
Drop at midnight if I don't fall asleep
First in Times Square on my television.
My planetarium tells me the universe
Is a scrum of stars and is rowdy as

Texas when I run out of gas and conviction
On a dark desert road in the middle of winter.
Once people thought there was music made by
The spheres, a calliope before iTunes and Spotify.
One thing you can count on with this universe—
Cherry-picking your friends, stupid universe,
Turning them into dust and decomposing memories.
Here's my hat, universe, what's your hurry?
You shouldn't eat a plate of hard-boiled eggs
At a single setting, the least of my problems.
The most of my problems: the racket above,
Furniture being rearranged by the insomniacs
Upstairs, like they can't wait for sunrise,
Which I get, what's the use waiting on this universe?
Deepak, I'm tired of this tired universe and its laws,
Its nasty little secrets, same jokes it does not know
How to tell, how my energy is hardly conserved,
How entropy possesses a primitive appeal.
I was wondering if you'll ever come back, pay the rent,
Pick up the belongings you left behind. Then I looked
In your boxes, saw all of my stuff was yours.

# MY MISSION STATEMENT

*To bring inspiration and innovation to every*
*athlete in the world.*
—*Nike's mission statement*

My mission is to be a unique driving experience.
My mission is to be putty in your hands.
My mission is to be your favorite pair of jeans.
My mission is to whisper in your ear in
Several pre-selected Romance languages. To star
In a movie that takes Sundance by storm.
(I hope Penelope Cruz will be in it
Even though she will contractually throw pans
Of ink on my head and shoot me colorfully
With a sleepy pistol and make her lips do that
Pouty thing upon which we can hang
*The Collected Works of Henry James.*)
Which reminds me. My mission is
To rewrite the dull parts of the *Kama Sutra.*
Because, listen, people! What's a man without a dream?
I say he's calamari soup. I say he's a man without
A mission statement. This is why my mission
Is to be a global partner and a preferred
Provider. To serve nutritious food to
A hungry world. To leave it all on the field,
To go hard when coach calls my number.

My mission is to write one thing you must
Slip under your pillow. My mission is:
Be the pillow. My mission is: Be the night.
My mission is to bring inspiration and innovation
To each recluse in town, to every space
Station captain, to all radio listeners too shy
To call in, to even the stranger who left a nice note
On my windshield that time. You know who you are.
My mission is, be in business forever.

## ACKNOWLEDGMENTS

Thank you, Patti James.

Thank you, Don Bogen, Laura Cogan, Kim Dower, Diane Frank, Beth Spencer.

Thank you, Dean Young.

The author also thanks the editors of publications in which these poems first appeared:

*88*
"End of an Age"

*The American Reader*
"My Last Résumé"
"The Ringling Bros Barnum and My Family Circus"

*The Cincinnati Review*
"The Satrap Will See You Now"

*Forklift, Ohio*
"Sleep Is/Is Not a Lost Cause"
"Plums of My Imaginary Daughter" [#18 "Brief Biography of an Imaginary Daughter"]

*Poetry Daily*
"Adventures in Language School"

*Zyzzyva*
"Adventures in Language School"

"I Was Just Leaving"

"More Elements of Style"

"My Mission Statement"

"Reasons Nobody Ever Called a Good Book of Poems a
Page-Turner"

"Symptomatology"

"There Comes a Time There Comes a Time, Or: Go Forth"

*Rivers of Earth and Sky: Poems for the 21st Century*
(Blue Light Press):
"My Mission Statement"